Dudley Pippin's Summer

DUDLEY PIPPIN'S SUMMER

Philip Ressner

pictures by Ben Shecter

HARPER & ROW, PUBLISHERS

New York, Hagerstown, San Francisco, London

For Arlene,
no kin to Dudley
but a pippin nevertheless

Dudley Pippin's Summer

Printed in the United States of America. For information address Harper & Row, Publishers, Inc., 10 East 53rd Street, New York, N.Y. 10022.
Published simultaneously in Canada by Fitzhenry & Whiteside Limited, Toronto.
FIRST EDITION

Library of Congress Cataloging in Publication Data
Ressner, Philip.
Dudley Pippin's summer.

SUMMARY: Eleven short stories recount Dudley Pippin's discoveries and adventures during a summer holiday.
[1. Vacations—Fiction] I. Shecter, Ben.
II. Title.
PZ7.R323Dx 1979 [E] 78-19831
ISBN 0-06-024887-4
ISBN 0-06-024888-2 lib. bdg.

Contents

Dudley and Half the World

Early on a morning in July, Dudley and his mother and father and the baby started for the country on their summer vacation. It was so early that the sun was only just beginning to light the edge of the world. The air was cool and smelled as if no one had breathed it yet. As far off as Dudley could see, there was no one; the streets were empty, waiting for the day.

"I bet we're the only people awake in the whole world," Dudley said as they drove off in their little blue car.

"Well," Dudley's mother said, "in *half* the world, anyway."

"Yes," his father said. "It's always night over half the world."

Dudley said, "But then the other half of the world would always be asleep."

"Pretty close to half," Dudley's father said. "Just think of it: half the people in the world stretched out and snoozing away."

"And half always wide awake," Dudley said.

Dudley's mother yawned. "Well, not always *wide* awake," she said.

Then everyone was quiet, and the car hummed along past dark and silent buildings and gardens, past hedges and doorways and empty schoolyards. Finally Dudley said, “It’s as if half the people of the world are always standing guard, taking care of things while the other half’s asleep.”

Then he rolled down the window and put his head out. The air was like a cool, strong river pressing against his face. “It’s all right, everybody,” he yelled into the darkness. “We’re here; we’re watching.” And his words flew out into the streaming river of air and on with it as it circled the earth from dark side to light, and from light to dark, endlessly.

Dudley and the Farmer

Dudley was flying his yellow racing bike down the little back road that always smelled of the sea, when he saw Farmer Glumpke riding on a green tractor in a greener field. The old man had blue eyes and a long dumb face. Dudley circled a couple of times and then came in for a landing. "Hello," he said. "Is that fun?"

The old man stopped the tractor and thought for a while. "Was once," he said. "Now it's just pleasing."

Dudley got down from his bicycle. "What are you doing?" he asked.

"Helping my potato plants to grow," the farmer said.

Dudley said, "Will those plants really turn the dirt into potatoes?"

"Yep, plants turn dirt and sunshine into all *kinds* of things."

Dudley smelled the fresh night smell that came from the sunny earth. "It's like a trick," he said.

"It is," said the old man. "But people have a trick that's just as good; we turn *potatoes* into *us*."

"And we do it without knowing how," Dudley said.

"Keerect," said the old man. "And meanwhile, while we're waiting for the potatoes to grow, maybe we can get a start on turning these here two pippins into us." And he took two pale-pink apples out of his overalls and gave one to Dudley. Then they sat down under an old poplar tree, that some people call a cottonwood, and in the warm hollow of the late afternoon they ate the crackling apples and listened to the potatoes grow.

Dudley and Margot

One gray and foggy day, when the gulls were all poking around the beach looking for the sun, Dudley saw a girl called Margot walking with one foot in the water and one foot on the sand.

"My name's Dudley," Dudley said. "Do you want to be friends?"

"No," Margot said, kicking a little wave that gurgled around her ankle.

"How come?" Dudley said.

"Well," Margot said, "friends are a pain."

Dudley said, "A friend is somebody who likes you."

"A friend is somebody you have to get birthday presents for," Margot said. "And when they're sick, you have to ask them how they feel, and if they tell you, you have to listen. And you have to agree with

them when they have an argument with somebody. And all that kind of stuff."

"Do you have any friends?" Dudley asked.

Margot said, "Sarah, Judy, Max, Simon, Alice, Anabel, and Middleton, who's a city boy like you."

"Wow," Dudley said. "How come you have all those friends if friends are a pain?" He picked a little stone as gray as the fog out of the wet sand.

"Well," Margot said, "because I want somebody to remember my birthday, and agree with me, and ask me how I feel, and all that stuff." She kicked at another wave. "Say," she said, after a moment, "how about you be *my* friend, but I won't be yours?"

"Okay," Dudley said. "When's your birthday?"

"June thirtieth," Margot said.

"I'll remember," Dudley said. And then Margot went off down the beach. Soon she had disappeared into

the fog. But then, after a moment, Dudley heard her voice from far off out of the pearly grayness:

"Dudle-e-e . . ." she called, "when . . . is . . . *your* . . . birthday?"

Dudley and the Witch (No. 2)

One day Dudley and his orange dog Rollo were eating Oreos in the shade of a horse chestnut tree. A little witch came by in a pale-blue bathing suit. "I know you," said the witch. "You're the nice boy who gave me his coonskin cap that time I lost mine in the city."

"That's right," Dudley said. "Can you make me about thirty feet tall?"

The witch said, "Well, what for?"

"Well," Dudley said, "I'd like to be able to step over a little house or tree and things like that."

The witch thought for a moment. "How about," she said, "I make you really small instead? Smaller can

be very nice, you know; you can crawl under all kinds of things and you can surprise people and things like that."

"Nope," Dudley said. "I'd rather be bigger."

"Um," the witch said. "Well, how about invisible? That can *really* be fun."

Dudley said, "But I'd really rather be bigger. It makes a person feel special."

"Special!" The witch stamped her foot. "Everybody wants to be bigger," she yelled, "or faster, or smarter, or stronger, or whatever. Can't *everybody* be bigger, you know."

"Why not?" Dudley asked.

"Because," said the witch, "if nobody was smaller, then the big ones wouldn't have anyone to be bigger than."

“Well,” Dudley said, “maybe there could be just one small person for everybody else to be bigger than.”

“Then nobody would be able to feel special,” said the witch.

“Except the one person who was small,” Dudley said.

The witch thought for a while. “Then everyone would want to be small,” she said.

“Maybe,” Dudley said, “we'd better just leave everything the way it is.”

“Okay,” said the witch. “Let's go for a swim.”

“Okay,” Dudley said. “Bet I can swim faster than you.”

Dudley and the Cows

On a cool bright day that smelled like cucumbers, Dudley went for a stroll down the lane behind Farmer Glumpke's brown cow barn. He saw a black cow and a brown cow sitting together behind a fence. "Hello, cows," he said.

"Hello," answered the brown cow.

"Gosh," Dudley said. "How come you can talk?"

"Oh," the cow said, "it's probably a dream."

"Well," Dudley said, "what are you doing?"

"We're on our lunch hour," the cow said.

"But you're not eating anything."

"Of course not," she said. "We don't eat when it's lunchtime; eating is work."

44

Dudley said, “Farmer Glumpke was working the other day, and he said it was pleasing.”

“Mm,” the cow said. “Ever eat grass all day?”

“No,” Dudley said.

“Farmer Glumpke ever eat grass all day?”

“I don’t think so,” Dudley said.

“Well, then,” said the cow, getting to her feet, “let’s not have any more of this foolishness about how pleasing it is to eat grass.” Then she said to the black cow, “Come on, Wilma, let’s get back to work.” And the two cows started off.

Dudley climbed onto the fence. "But you *like* to eat grass," he called after them. "Everybody knows you cows like to eat grass."

The brown cow looked over her shoulder. "Nonsense," she said. "A person can't like something they do for a living."

"You're not a person," Dudley shouted.

The two cows stopped and looked at Dudley. "And you," the brown cow said, "are not a cow."

"Moo," said Wilma.

Dudley and the Elf

One day Dudley was exploring with the baby and found a cool wood deep down at the bottom of the hot meadow. An elf with a beard was sitting in one of the trees. "I'm Greapentrog," he said. "Want to sell that baby?"

"No," Dudley said.

"Blabl," said the baby.

Greapentrog looked sly out of the corner of his eyes. "I'll make you king," he said, "if you give me that baby."

Dudley shifted the baby to his other arm. "The United States of America doesn't have a king," he said. "And anyway, people don't buy and sell babies."

"Oh, is that so?" Greapentrog said. "Well, how did *you* get it then, I'd like to know?"

"I *didn't* get it," said Dudley. "It's my mother's. Why doesn't your mother get one of her own?"

"We elves don't *have* mothers," Greapentrog said.

Dudley thought for a moment. Then he said, "I guess if you don't have mothers, then there can't be any fathers either."

"Right," said Greapentrog. "No fathers."

"Then you're not families," Dudley said. "What are you then?"

Greapentrog thought about it. "Well, we're sort of a big bowling team."

"Oh," Dudley said. "What do you *do*?"

"Well," Greapentrog said, "we bowl a lot. What do families do?"

"Oh, we went bowling once," Dudley said. "We went to a movie last week."

Greapentrog looked jealous. "Yeah?" he said, kicking the tree with his heel. "Movies are bad for your eyes."

"Sometimes my mother or father gives us a hug and talks to us when we're sad," Dudley said. "Or they tell us a story when we go to bed."

Greapentrog stared off into the trees. He looked as if he might cry. "Babbik!" the baby said, reaching for him.

"And my grandfather took me on the Scrambler ride last month," Dudley continued. "And my grandmother makes warm rolls that she gives us, and she tells us about the old days."

Then nobody said anything for a while. Finally, Greapentrog said, "I rode on an eagle once."

Dudley said, "Gosh!"

"Yep," said the elf, twiddling his thumbs. "Well, three or four times, actually."

"Gosh," Dudley said again.

And then Greapentrog jumped down out of the tree. "Well," he said, "got a big game tonight; we're playing the Catskill Thunderballers. Got to get going." And he turned and walked off.

And Dudley stood and listened to the enormous silent green of the woods. And the baby breathed softly in his ear.

Dudley and the Horn Player

One sunny day Dudley heard a cow in the meadow across the road. It was a man playing a French horn. He was sitting in the clover, and the golden horn blazed in the light like another sun.

"Why are you playing a French horn?" Dudley asked.

The man was wearing green plaid shorts and had a nice tan. "Well," he said, "I tried the guitar, but I was always spraining my ankle when I practiced."

"Oh," Dudley said. "My mother had a saxophone once, but it had two keys broken. And she said she didn't want to play it anyhow, because it sounded sad."

"Oh, I see," the man said. "I hope she's feeling more cheerful now."

"Well, it wasn't *her* that was sad," Dudley said.

"Oh," said the man. "Who *was* it that was sad?"

Dudley sat down and chewed a piece of clover for a while. It didn't sound right, but he said, "It was the saxophone."

The man put down his horn. "Well, that beats everything," he said. "A saxophone with feelings."

"No!" Dudley yelled. "It *sounded* sad. . . ." The man peered at Dudley. ". . . to my mother," Dudley finished quietly.

The man tootled softly on his horn, but he said nothing.

"Well," Dudley said, after a bit, "I guess it *was* my mother had the sad feelings; things don't have feelings."

"Well, hooray for that," said the man. "Where would we be without feelings?"

Then he and Dudley marched single file round and round the meadow while he played a loud tune that would have sounded joyful to anyone who was ready to be.

And a brown cow put her silken face over the fence and watched them sadly.

Dudley and Mrs. Alippo

One bright, blue-sky morning Dudley went to Alippo's General Store to buy the Sunday paper. Mrs. Alippo was sitting at the counter having a nice cup of tea. Everything smelled of cloves and raincoats.

Dudley said, "Hello, Mrs. Alippo."

Mrs. Alippo was old and a little deaf. "Ah," she said, "it's not like the old country."

"Was everything great there?" Dudley asked.

"Nah," Mrs. Alippo said, "but you could always get a good cuppa tea."

Dudley pointed at her cup. "Isn't that good?" he asked.

"Nice," Mrs. Alippo said, "but not good."

"What's the difference?" asked Dudley.

"Well," Mrs. Alippo said, "*nice* is tasty and hot; *good* is tasty and hot and a cozy room with mauve wallpaper and maybe a little fog outside so you can only just barely make out the iron gate of the house across the road."

Dudley said, "But can't you have a good cuppa tea on a sunny day?"

"Oh, yes," Mrs. Alippo said, "but then it has to be with two old friends in a kitchen with a blue-tile floor and a door onto a little garden."

"Oh," Dudley said. "A garden is nice."

"And good," said Mrs. Alippo. "*Nice* is green grass and a white fence; *good* is grass and a fence and a horse chestnut tree with prickly pale-green chestnuts and a shady corner in the tall grass next to the mossy wall where you can sit and have a long private talk after school with your friend Myra."

"Was Myra nice?" Dudley asked.

Mrs. Alippo said, "Yes, *nice* was Myra; *good* was her brother Claude and the little bouquet of pansies with purple velvet centers that he gave me on my fourteenth birthday and who I loved ever since."

Then Mrs. Alippo called to Mr. Alippo, who was putting some orange sugar peanuts into a bag for a little girl in a Texaco suit. "Claude," she said, "I think this nice boy wants his Sunday paper."

"*Good* boy," Dudley said.

44

Dudley and the Auction

One windy, starlit night that made you want to run down the dark road and jump at the sky, Dudley went with his parents to an auction. It was in a hot, crowded barn full of old furniture, books, junk, and people.

The auctioneer, who was selling the things, stood on a box at one end of the barn. In no time he had talked people into buying an old chest of drawers with no drawers, an old two-handled saw, and a box of old yellowed dishes with little blue flowers around their edges that some people had probably eaten out of fifty times a thousand times.

"Why do people want all those old, used things?" Dudley asked.

"Well, some of them are beautiful," his father said.

"And some of them are useful," his mother said.

"What about the rest of them?" Dudley asked.

His father said, "*All* those things remind us of all the people who lived in the world before us."

"Then someday," Dudley said, "maybe a hundred years from now, somebody might buy the baby's cradle or my yellow cocoa mug and keep it on a shelf and look at it and wonder who *we* were?"

"Or even *my* old cocoa mug, that I still have and that has a picture of Orphan Annie on it," Dudley's father said.

AUCTION
RULES

"Or my yellow bicycle," Dudley's mother said. "Or the green porcelain flowerpot with the handles."

"And they'll think about us," Dudley said, "and how we must have once used all those things."

"Yes," Dudley's mother said, "even though they never knew us or even our names."

"Who'll give me ten dollars for this beautiful old mirror?" said the auctioneer, holding up a beautiful old mirror.

"Bet that old mirror has reflected a million things," Dudley's father said, and held up his hand. "Five dollars," he called to the auctioneer.

"First thing when I get home," Dudley said, "I'm going to put my name on the bottom of my yellow mug."

Dudley and the Blueberries

Dudley and Middleton were picking blueberries near the stone wall that ran along the edge of the woods down by the railroad tracks. It took five years to half fill Dudley's mother's white pot that had a big chip that looked like the inside of an oyster shell.

"This takes a long time," Dudley said. It was hot.

"Uh-huh," Middleton said.

They picked for two more years and Middleton said, "This takes a long time."

"Uh-huh," Dudley said.

Three years later, when the pot was almost full, Margot came zipping along the top of the stone wall in her orange dee-dah sneakers.

"We just picked a thousand million blueberries," Middleton said.

Margot said, "Those are chokecherries. Only birds eat them."

"But they're blue," Middleton said. "And they're berries."

Margot pointed over the wall. "*Those* are blueberries," she said.

"But they're red," Dudley said.

"Well," Margot said, "blueberries are red when they're green."

Nobody said anything for a moment. Then Dudley said, "How can they be green *and* red?"

"That's right," Middleton said. "How come?"

Margot yelled, "They're red *because* they're green."

Dudley started to laugh. "When greenberries are redberries," he yelled, "they're blueberries."

"No," Margot screamed, jumping up and down. "When something isn't ripe, you say it's *green.* So if they weren't green, they would be blue, you dodoes."

Middleton was dancing with the pot on his head. "Oh, when the bluegreenies are reddies," he sang, "they're not."

Dudley took Middleton's arm, and together they danced around Margot, singing. Middleton sang, "When redbellies are brune, they're gleen." And Dudley sang, "Oh, when breenjellies are glue, they're renge." Then he and Middleton carefully dumped the whole pot of berries over Margot's head, and Margot went home.

Dudley and the Last Day

The mattress on Dudley's bed was rolled up like a Yodel. Margot was bouncing on the springs while Dudley packed to go home to the city.

"How about," she said, "you stay here always?"

"I can't do that," Dudley said.

"It's so nice in the country, I don't see why everybody doesn't live here all the time," Margot said.

"Well," Dudley said, "if they did, then the country would be the city."

"How come?" Margot said. She put her feet on the wall and hung her head upside down over the edge of the bed.

"You dummy," Dudley said. "Because then everybody would be *here*, and a city is a lot of people in one place."

"I love it when you call me a dummy," Margot said.

Dudley said, "But I never called you a dummy before."

"I know," Margot said. "But a girl said that once in a movie."

"Movies are bad for your eyes," Dudley said.

"Oh, poo; who said so?"

"Greapentrog," Dudley said.

Margot was beginning to feel bad. She didn't want Dudley to leave. "Greapentrog," she hooted. "What a

name! Does he live in the dumb city too? What are you doing with that doll?"

"It's not a doll," Dudley said. "It's a GI Joe."

"It's a *doll*," Margot said, laughing a dirty laugh. "Hoo-hoo, Dudley plays with dolls, oh, hoo-ha-hoo."

"What's wrong with that anyway?" Dudley said.

Margot said, "You're too *old* for dolls, that's what."

"You're never too old for dolls," Dudley said.

"Well," Margot yelled, "*I'm* not going to play with anybody who plays with dolls."

"That's right," Dudley said, "because I'm not going to be here anymore." Then Margot began to cry, and ran out of the room. Through his window Dudley saw her run down the road. Then his mother called him. He zipped up his bag and took it out to the car.

As they started off, Dudley saw Margot far off across the meadow. She was running toward them. "Dudle-e-e . . ." she called. Her voice was tiny and frail, already slipping away into autumn. Then, again, very faint: "Dudle-e-e . . . you're not . . . too old . . . for dolls."

And then, so far away: "Dudle-e-e . . . come back."